Paul Cézanne

Detail from Plate I.

Funk & Wagnalls, Inc., New York

ELLEN H. JOHNSON
PROFESSOR OF ART, OBERLIN COLLEGE, OBERLIN, OHIO

Paul Cézanne 1839-1906

Paul Cézanne was born on **January 19, 1839**, at Aix-en-Provence, the son of Louis-Auguste Cézanne, a prosperous hat merchant who later became a banker. In 1858 Paul graduated from **the Collège Bourbon**, where he received a solid classical education and where he began his long friendship with Emile Zola. The two boys spent their summers reading, writing poetry and roaming the countryside together. Cézanne's love of the land remained with him, gradually maturing into a passionate devotion. While at school, he also attended classes at the Ecole des Beaux-Arts, which was connected with the municipal museum. Submitting to his father's wishes, Cézanne studied law at the University of Aix from 1859 to early 1861.

In 1859 his father purchased a country estate, the Jas de Bouffan, whose noble house and gardens often appear in Cézanne's mature paintings.

Cézanne's desire to prove that he could make a financial success of painting probably caused him at least as much anguish as did his father's early refusal to allow him to become a professional painter; and this need, still unfulfilled at his father's death in 1886, was related to Cézanne's lasting hope for official recognition. Year after year he continued to submit paintings to the Salon although he could only anticipate rejection of his shockingly unorthodox work. Partly through the intercession of his sympathetic mother but primarily through the patient and enthusiastic encouragement of Zola, who had moved to Paris in 1858, Cézanne persevered, until in April, 1861, he finally gained permission from his father for go to Paris to study art. Apparently failing to qualify for admission to the Ecole des Beaux-Arts, he worked at the Académie Suisse, where he met **Pissarro, who became for him** 'a man to be consulted—something like God'.

For the next twenty years he was active much of the time in and around Paris, although he never liked to stay too long away from his 'good sun of **Provence**', which even Van Gogh did not love more deeply than he. He continued his self-education by studying and copying at the Louvre and the Trocadéro. In 1863 he exhibited at the historic Salon des Refusés. Having become friends with Monet, Renoir and the other young rebels who revered Manet, he found himself a member of the avant-garde during the formative years of Impressionism. In 1869 he met Hortense Fiquet but she did not legally become his wife until 1886. His son Paul, for whom he always had the deepest affection, was born in 1872.

Between 1872 and 1882, he frequently stayed at Auvers and Pontoise, where he worked with Pissarro, the Impressionist from whom he learned most and with whom he had the most in common. In 1874 the three paintings which he exhibited in the first Impressionist exhibition were cruelly ridiculed. However, even from the beginning his work was highly regarded by his colleagues and by a few far-sighted amateurs.

In 1877 Cézanne exhibited with the Impressionists for the last time, partly because the notoriety and persistently unfavourable popular criticism his work provoked were too painful and distracting. From 1877 until his first one-man exhibition at Vollard's gallery in 1895 his work was very little seen by the public, who thought of him—if at all—as the mad hermit of Aix. Although Cézanne was in Paris less frequently and for shorter periods after about 1882, he continued to go there throughout his life to visit friends, paint portraits and study at the Louvre. Constantly moving about, up and down the country, he seldom remained long in Aix; but he always had his base there. His mother having died in 1897, Cézanne sold the Jas de Bouffan in 1899 and moved to 23 rue Boulegon in Aix. In 1902 he also had a studio built on the Chemin des Lauves, looking out over the city and away to the mountain.

Apart from the paintings which knowledgeable critics and collectors could see at Père Tanguy's art shop, the occasions on which his pictures were included in public exhibitions from 1877 to 1895 were extremely few. However, he came again to public notice—and again suffered abuse—in 1886 with the publication of Zola's 'L'Oeuvre' whose hero, a failed painter driven to suicide, was identified with Cézanne. Though the appearance of the novel may have played some part in his break with Zola, there were other causes. Cézanne felt uncomfortable and not altogether welcome in the home of Mme Zola; but, above all, the novelist never really understood the painter's work.

Very few of Cézanne's friendships could withstand his difficult nature: neurotically sensitive, he imagined insult or the violation of his privacy when neither was intended; he was profoundly ill-at-ease in society; and almost no one was safe from his outbursts of temper. His irascibility was fundamentally linked to his need for solitude, not because he was a misanthrope but indeed because he was so painfully responsive to other people; and above all because solitude was essential for his work. As he wrote to his son shortly before his death, 'My life arranged in this way allows me to isolate myself from the lower spheres of life.'

Old and ill, he continued to work incessantly. On August 26, 1906, in the 'stupefying' heat of the late summer, he wrote to Paul that he had stayed in bed late that morning, until after five o'clock, a time at which he was usually hard at work in his studio on the Chemin des Lauves. On October 15, caught in a storm while painting, he collapsed and was brought home; but the next morning he was again at work. He died on October 22, 1906.

In the last decade of his life critical acclaim increased, and his work was more and more in demand for purchase and exhibition; several young painters and writers openly venerated him and came to him for advice. Nevertheless, he could not still his uncertainty and the dread that he would never, as he wrote in 1905, 'realize the dream of art that I have been pursuing all my life.'

This very doubt is at the heart of Cézanne's meaning for many of the painters who followed him. For Picasso, 'It's not what the artist does that counts, but what he is. Cézanne would never have interested me a bit if he had lived and thought like Jacques Emile Blanche, even if the apple he painted had been ten times as beautiful. What compels our interest is Cézanne's anxiety—that's Cézanne's lesson . . .' And Matisse, referring to a painting by Cézanne which he had owned since 1899, wrote in 1936, 'It has sustained me spiritually in the critical moments of my career as an artist; from it I have drawn my faith and perseverance.'

'I owe you the truth in painting.' — CÉZANNE

CÉZANNE'S NEVER-ENDING, humble and heroic search for truth is the moral condition of his art and a primary source of its greatness. His truth, like Wordsworth's, is the truth of art 'in the keeping of the senses'. In his faithfulness both to nature and to art, his synthesis of minute visual sensation with a grandeur of formal construction, Cézanne stands alone. Austere and difficult of access as his work may be on first encounter, prolonged contemplation slowly reveals his delicate exactitude and the depth of his feeling for nature, which to him meant 'man, woman, and still-life' as well as landscape.

Although Cézanne almost never dated his paintings and it is difficult to assign dates to them with precision, certain crucial changes serve to divide his work into a few fairly distinct phases. The early paintings, of the 1860's, are violent expressions of his dark, tortured imagination, his unfulfilled eroticism, and the anxieties springing from the repressive hand of his father and from his own despair of realizing the grandeur of his dreams. Such themes as the temptation of St. Anthony, rape, murder and even the portraits, picnics, landscapes, still lifes and the translations from other art, are painted with brutal power. They can also be as astonishingly elegant as the *Still-Life with Black Clock* (Stavros S. Niarchos, Paris). Crude and even grotesque as the youthful paintings have appeared to some critics, they are monumental pre-Expressionist images whose dramatic contrasts of black and white intensify the red, blue or green areas and whose dense surfaces, tempestuously built up with the brush and knife, harken back to Goya and herald De Kooning. Clearly Cézanne's early painting owes much to Delacroix, and the characteristically sensuous paint in *Man in a Blue Cap* (Plate I) even exceeds that of another of his masters, Courbet.

This *couillarde* technique, as Cézanne termed it, was abandoned in his Impressionist phase, which began in about 1872 when he made the first of several visits to Auvers and Pontoise. Here, in close association with Pissarro, he learned to relate his painting more to the evidence of his eyes and to register what he saw by means of short, separate strokes of fresh colour. That this shift in direction from interior to exterior vision was of decisive importance in developing what he called his 'own means of expression' was attested to when, exhibiting in Aix a few years before he died, he designated himself 'pupil of Pissarro'.

Although none of the *plein air* painters examined the relationship between colour and light more exhaustively than did Cézanne, his analysis never led him to abandon the full volume of objects and the firmly constructed space which he admired in the art of the past. These qualities are apparent in his earliest Impressionist paintings, notably *The House of the Hanged Man* (Plate III) of c. 1873, as well as in the work from the end of the decade, such as *The Château of Médan* (Plate IV), where the foliage and even its reflection in the Seine are as substantially constructed as the buildings. During the next few years he placed the little parallel blocks of paint with ever-increasing exacti-

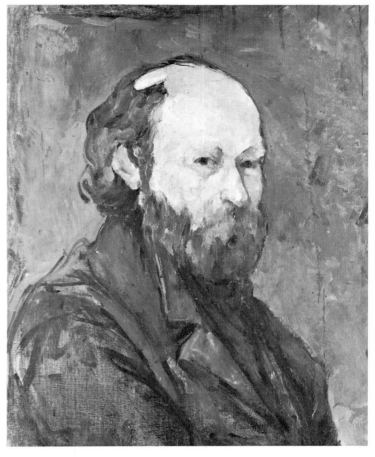

1. SELF-PORTRAIT (c. 1877)
The Phillips Collection, Washington, D.C.

tude to record his sensations of colour, volume and space, as they moved, series after series, in changing directions corresponding to and enforcing the structure and growth of the object and its directional force in the painting. Indeed, in several of the paintings from the early 1880's, he modelled volumes and thrust them out into space as securely as though he were chiselling them from rock. One would think that Cézanne might have been a sculptor, were it not that his mighty forms and the space they occupy are built up by means of colour in subtle inter-action.

Later in the 1880's Cézanne had gained sufficient command of his *petites sensations* to be able to relax a little the stern regimenting of the colour strokes. The looser, thinner and more open painting of *Mont Sainte-Victoire* (Plate VIII) brings an expansive space which allows the forms to breathe more easily. The mass of the mountain is constructed by subtle modulations of colour, from blue to violet to pink to orange to ochre to green. Each variation in colour creates a different indentation or projection of the form which corresponds so precisely to the actual contours of the mountain that one can identify the exact angle from which each of the more than sixty pictures of Mont Sainte-Victoire was made. The fact that Cézanne could represent exactly the form of objects is of no importance in itself; but it is significant that he wanted to, and did, maintain the identity of individual objects at the same time as he adjusted and bent them to his creative will. In this particular painting he has made the form of the garden wall echo the slant of the fields which fan out from the house, and he has brought into rhythmic accord the arcs and angles of the branches of the tree, the mountain and the valley. He has almost completely dispensed with the texture of objects in favour of the unifying texture of the paint. In the valley the distinction between green and orange-ochre induces a sensation of different locations in space. At the same time, these green and orange planes are decisively shaped in relation to the rectangular format of the picture and, even though they are slanting rectangles moving in zig-zag directions to suggest the extension of the valley, they are also flat, conforming to the essential nature of the picture plane. Moreover, the green planes tend to move back while the recurring orange-ochre areas come forward, and the colour intensity, unlike that in traditional illusionist paint-

2. STUDY OF A FIGURE (AFTER RUBENS)
Kunstmuseum, Basel

ing, diminishes very little, if at all, in the distance. By these and far more carefully contemplated means, the illusion of space and volume is firmly presented—and as firmly denied. The represented reality gives way to the created reality; but Cézanne never conceals the tension between the two in his insistence on the truth of both. Already here, in the 1880's, he laid down that premise of his art on which so much of twentieth-century art has been built.

Cézanne's insistence on the truth of feeling was no less strongly maintained. However, the emotions expressed, in keeping with the complexity and contradictions of his nature, his mind and his work, are neither simple nor single. In the *Mont Sainte-Victoire* painting, tranquil and buoyant as it is, one senses something of 'the struggle for life' which Van Gogh found in the 'living being' of trees; but trying to put words to such feelings is so hopeless that one can only conclude, as Cézanne did, 'it is better to feel them'.

Cézanne's painting is born of the senses and addresses itself directly to them. Looking at this picture of Mont Sainte-Victoire from Montbriant on his brother-in-law's estate 'Bellevue', one experiences again the sensation of the clear, dry air and burning sun of Provence and the trees whipping in the wind; and one vividly recalls the green fields and the orange earth which, from miles away, can be seen to move up into the blue and violet rock of the mountain. But Cézanne's art is also born of what he called 'the logic of organized sensations'. He is reported to have said that he wanted 'to make of Impressionism something as solid and enduring as the art of the museums' and that the kind of 'classic' effect which he sought was 'Poussin remade entirely after nature'. Comparing Cézanne's painting with that of Poussin, one recognizes a similar reasoning at work in the monumental simplification, the elimination of the fortuitous, the geometric decisiveness of forms and the precisely calculated distances between them. These are among the elements which contribute to the grave serenity that pervades the painting of both masters. However, Cézanne weds this idealism with the scientific materialism to which the Impressionists adhered more closely. Using their analytical method of perceptual painting, he created his profoundly intellectual and universal 'ideal of art' not outside of but within and from the framework of specific observation. To many of his contemporary critics Cézanne seemed to be the great destroyer of the classical tradition. In reality, as we now see, he, like Seurat, was one of its great restorers. There were, however, a few critics who responded to the classical quality of his work. Georges Rivière, as early as 1877, called Cézanne 'a Greek of the great period' and those who ridiculed his work 'barbarians criticizing the Parthenon'.

In his still life paintings Cézanne achieved a similar harmony between the perception of nature and the logic of form. The painted apples, bottles, flowers, bread and even tablecloths appear as everlasting and unmoving as his mountain. One does not expect to find a still life of ordinary objects so monumental and grave as the *Still Life with Basket of Apples* (Plate X) unquestionably is. This quietude, however, is like that suggested by T.S. Eliot's line, 'At the still point of the turning world'. The individual objects seem to move, shift, expand and contract as though possessed of a magical life of their own.

The problem of representing three-dimensional objects in space on a two-dimensional surface is as old as painting; but Cézanne's solution to that problem fundamentally questions the concept of space which for centuries had prevailed in western art. According to the laws of linear perspective formulated in the Renaissance, all the objects in a picture are represented as though seen from a single, fixed, static point. Cézanne, subjecting objects to the demands of their pictorial relationships, introduced multiple and moving view-points. In the *Still Life with Basket of Apples* the biscuits appear as though seen from the left and above as well as *en face*. The top two biscuits are suspended beyond their support, curiously increasing the sensation of their amplitude of form. The oval of the plate is squared off like the biscuits, relating these shapes to other oval and rectangular forms; the basket and its handle, the apples and the colour planes which model them are pulled towards the shape of the picture itself in a complex oval-rectangle counterpoint. The left side of the table is completely flat, not viewed from any single position; it gives pictorial but no conceivable physical support for the swelling basket of fruit, within which the scale of the apples changes considerably. By enlarging, simplifying and flattening forms towards the outer parts of the composition, Cézanne accentuates, by contrast, the fuller volumes and more quickly changing colours, shapes and lines in the central parts (a compositional arrangement often followed in Cubist paintings). The left edges of the table do not correspond to those on the right; these discrepancies set up a pictorial tug-of-war concealed by the cloth and the bottle and basket. (The Cubists would remove the cloth.) We *feel* these tensions and we feel the slanting bottle straining away from the axes of the biscuits. Through this empathy we experience the life and evolution of the picture, and we marvel at the miraculously quiet but vibrant equilibrium which Cézanne creates from the conflicting forces in the still life.

In compelling the objects 'to put up with', in Picasso's phrase, the pictorial life which the artist assigns to them, Cézanne prepared the way for the Cubist fragmentation of the object and its eventual elimination in abstract painting. At the same time, while impelling our perception of the painting as painting, he heightens illusion. Cézanne's departures from traditional perspective more nearly approximate to the way in which we actually see with successive, shifting focus than does the Renaissance 'rationalization of sight', as perspective has been called. His slow and deliberate painting presents the experience of space in time—not the moment of the Impressionists, but time itself—as duration. The tensions and continuous interweavings between space and surface, volume and plane, near and far, create a fluctuating and dynamic relativity which suggests a parallel with modern concepts of time/space as an entity, neither any longer separate and independent from each other.

But apart from these implications of Cézanne's work there is its sheer beauty. The *Still Life with Plaster Cupid* (Plate XV) is a perfect harmony of consonant and dissonant elements, of related and opposing colour and of pointed shapes and swinging curves. The complex and daring zig-zag rhythm up and back into space reaches its climax in the expanded apple shape suspended breathlessly over the upward sweeping tilt of the floor. The qualities of objects are modified in accordance with the demands of the painting: the canvas behind the cupid curves to receive and conform to its forms; the section of another painting on the upper right is treated like a piece of relief sculpture; the green foreground apple forces the plate to give way to its coloured shape; objects throw

3. COAT ON CHAIR (c. 1890-1900)
Mrs. Marianne Feilchenfeldt, Zurich

green, blue, red or violet transparent shadows; the freely moving line strikes an accent here, a full contour there, and sometimes forms the object in complete independence from it. This fresh and beautiful still life is 'about' art: an actual cast of a piece of Baroque sculpture, a painting of another piece of sculpture, a canvas with no visible composition on it, the back of at least one more canvas leaning against the wall, and a section of a painted still life, whose cascading drapery spills out over the 'real' table. The new reality of painting which Cézanne creates, transcends and shatters the traditional distinctions between real and unreal or the different levels of reality.

One might say that the *Still Life with Apples and Oranges* (Plate XVI) is about opulence. Painted in Cézanne's last decade, it has the rich, saturated colour, the elaboration of design, and the grand Baroque movements which he could now allow himself. It also has a hint, perhaps in the smouldering intensity of colour, of the sombre mood which one often encounters in his late work. Sybaritic and forbidding, it bespeaks the abundance of the earth, and the terrors within it.

In his portraits Cézanne seeks and reveals the grave, silent dignity at the core of each human being. In spite of their basic immobility (to Vollard he shouted, 'You must sit like an apple! Does an apple move?'), his portraits have a formal vitality akin to the still lifes, but less complex. The immobility of Madame Cézanne's pose (Plate IX), as though she had been seated there forever, is qualified and enlivened by the slight but concentrated tension between the axis of her body and the slant of the chair on which she sits.

His portraits, and the figure compositions of card players and bathers, all have a solemn grandeur. This is particularly marked in *The Large Bathers* (Plate V-VI), a composition on which he worked for several years, painting three large versions and many smaller studies. The male bather groups, which he also painted but never in large format, are looser in their organisation with horizontal bands open at the sides in contrast to the usually closed-in, triangular disposition of the female groups. To paint an heroic-sized composition of bathers in the open air was a challenge which Cézanne's life-long devotion to nature and the grand tradition of art imposed upon him. Although his landscapes are almost invariably devoid of human figures, the theme of bathers in nature had preoccupied him since his student days. It was not, however, until the last decade of his life that he attempted to develop this theme on an imposing scale. He pursued it stubbornly in spite of great handicaps: failing health, the difficulty of moving the huge canvases out of doors and the impossibility of getting suitable models in provincial Aix. The idea came in part from his nostalgia for the days when he and his boyhood friends bathed in the Arc River under the large trees which, as he wrote to his son, 'form a vault over the water'. The sources of his figures were his student drawings and the studies he had made from Ancient, Renaissance and Baroque art, which he continued to copy even in his old age.

While the small bather paintings are more immediately appealing, each time one stands before *The Large Bathers* one responds anew to the majesty of its conception and the beauty of its execution. Both epic and idyllic, Olympian and Arcadian, it is Cézanne's dream of a pure state in nature. The sex of the figures has no more importance here than it has in Giotto's frescoes at Padua. Although the felicity of the actual painting may not be fully apparent from reproductions, its archaic grace is unmistakable. The severe architecture of its interlocking triangles is modified by sonorous arcs and more quickly changing curves; and the painting is extraordinarily complex and subtle in its trembling nuances of blue and ochre intermingled with many tints of orange, red, rose, lavender, green, brushed on in transparent and semi-transparent overlays of colour. The supple line ripples, curves, sharply squares itself off, disappears, multiplies itself, defines or slices across or runs outside the coloured shapes as it rides on its own free rhythm. The master has so fully conquered 'the knowledge of the means of expressing emotion' which, as he wrote in 1904, 'is only to be acquired through very long experience' that he is able to maintain in this monumental composition the lyricism and refinement of his less heroic painting and to endow it with a noble sentiment.

Like Monet, Cézanne gave full expression in his late landscapes to his deep feeling for the mysterious inner force of nature. The *élan vital* ("life force") celebrated by the philosopher Henri Bergson animates each rock and tree, each sweeping line, each plane of colour as surely as it does in the more overtly Expressionist painting of Van Gogh. In *Cabanon du Jourdan* (Riccardo Jucker Collection, Milan) the heaving earth, the chopping strokes of the brush, and the intense orange burning against brilliant blue convey his passion with equal eloquence. This compelling image has the same strangely foreboding expression as does the *Still Life with Apples and Oranges*.

A similar deepening of emotional expression occurs in the water-colour medium, which, from the middle of the 1870's, was closely related to the development of Cézanne's oil painting and is as richly varied. In some of the water-colours, by applying only a few transparent patches of colour over quick little pencil strokes he not only creates the illusion of palpable space occupied by solid volumes but he also makes a brilliantly coherent formal structure. Others are more densely built up, layer after layer like transparent sheets of coloured ice (Fig. 4). Line and colour weave in and around and under each other, setting in motion angular, curving and sweeping rhythms.

But even the freest water-colours hardly prepare one for the last *Mont Sainte-Victoire* oil paintings (Plate XI-XII) which are almost abstract in their daring reduction and transformation of visual sensation to the pulsating life of colour, line and shape. The faceted planes collide and multiply 'like a shell bursting into fragments which are again shells', to use the image by which Bergson described life. If one covers over the mountain, the rest of the picture could be an Abstract Expressionist painting. However, the mountain remains in its abiding majesty; as one looks at it, the valley falls into place and the small blocks of colour again assume their dual role.

Although Cézanne's innovations anticipated Cubism and subsequent abstraction, he only opened the gate to a garden which he had no thought of entering. His spiritual as well as physical vision remained firmly anchored in nature. As he wrote in 1896, 'were it not that I love excessively the configurations of my country, I would not be here.' The pictures which Cézanne painted in his slow and probing contemplation of nature demand our unhurried study. They do not give up their wonders easily or quickly; but they never exhaust them.

4. RIVER AT THE BRIDGE OF TROIS SAUTETS (1906)
Cincinnati Art Museum, Cincinnati, Ohio

I. MAN IN A BLUE CAP (UNCLE DOMINIC) (1865–66)
Oil on canvas. 31⅜ in. x 25¼ in.
Metropolitan Museum of Art, New York

Cézanne's early portraits were chiefly grave, monumental studies of himself, his father and uncle and his mistress, later Mme Cézanne. Between 1865 and 1867, during visits home to Aix, he did nine differently costumed portraits of his mother's brother Dominic Aubert, a bailiff. Here, Uncle Dominic's penetrating gaze and sober expression, which resemble those of Cézanne's self-portraits, may reflect the artist's early emotional turmoil and morose view of life.

The paint—typically black and earth colours—is applied heavily, almost violently, with a palette knife to produce dramatic lines and a sculptural, three-dimensional effect. The work is anchored, however, by the calm stability of its pyramidal construction, based on Dominic's coat and vest with its apex in his tasselled, blue-green cap. The central streak of black vest and the inverted triangle formed by his white shirt and red tie draw attention to his vigourously modelled face. Cézanne borrowed this compositional device, which he used in many works, from Titian and Velázquez, whom he continually returned to study in the Louvre.

II. A MODERN OLYMPIA (1872–73)
Oil on canvas. 18⅛ in. x 21⅞ in.
Louvre, Paris

In his four versions of the courtesan Olympia, done in the 1870's, Cézanne expressed both his unfulfilled erotic fantasies and his grudging respect for Edouard Manet, the leader of the avantgarde, who had painted a controversial Olympia ten years earlier. This version, the second, was painted while Cézanne was staying in Auvers. When his new friend, the eccentric physician Paul-Ferdinand Gachet, highly praised the Manet work, Cézanne, abandoning his usual labourious approach, dashed off his own Olympia. At the first Impressionist exhibition in 1874, it aroused great outcry because of its undisguised sensuality and exuberantly loose technique.

As a boorish, unkempt provincial in Paris, Cézanne was frightened of women and ill at ease with Manet's gentlemanly dress and polished manners. In this somewhat self-deprecating parody he portrays himself as a formally attired bourgeois gazing appreciatively at a coy courtesan being dramatically unveiled before him by her negro maid. Unlike Manet's poised, reclining nude, Cézanne's Olympia is childishly curled up, regarding her client with a seductive smile. The light, bright colours and free, sketchy brush strokes, seen in the flower-filled urn and the lavender sofa and drapery, are evidence of Cézanne's work with the Impressionist Pissarro the preceding summer.

III. THE HOUSE OF THE HANGED MAN (*c*. 1873)
Oil on canvas. 21⅝ in. x 26 in.
Louvre, Paris

In early 1872 Cézanne was living morosely in a poor, noisy flat in Paris, alienated from his friends, unable to support his mistress and newborn son Paul and anxiously searching for a personal painting style. That summer he gladly accepted the invitation of Pissarro to bring his family to Pontoise, in the Oise Valley. There Pissarro, a kindly, sensible older man, welcomed the young painter to his home and gave the undisciplined Cézanne the instruction he so badly needed.

Painting the tranquil countryside of Pontoise and nearby Auvers beside his fatherly mentor, whom he regarded as 'something like the Good Lord', Cézanne learned the Impressionist virtues of painting landscape directly in the open (*en plein air*) instead of in a studio, as was usual at that time. He also learned to lighten his palette and use short, broken brush strokes of pure unmixed colour that caught the effect of light on fields, foliage and other textured surfaces. *The House of the Hanged Man* is perhaps the first work to show this Impressionist influence. Pissarro, however, wisely never tried to force on Cézanne the Impressionists' overriding concern with the observation of changing surface effects. Cézanne sought the immutable underlying structure of natural forms, seen here in the controlled interplay of verticals and diagonals in the trees, walls, road and gables.

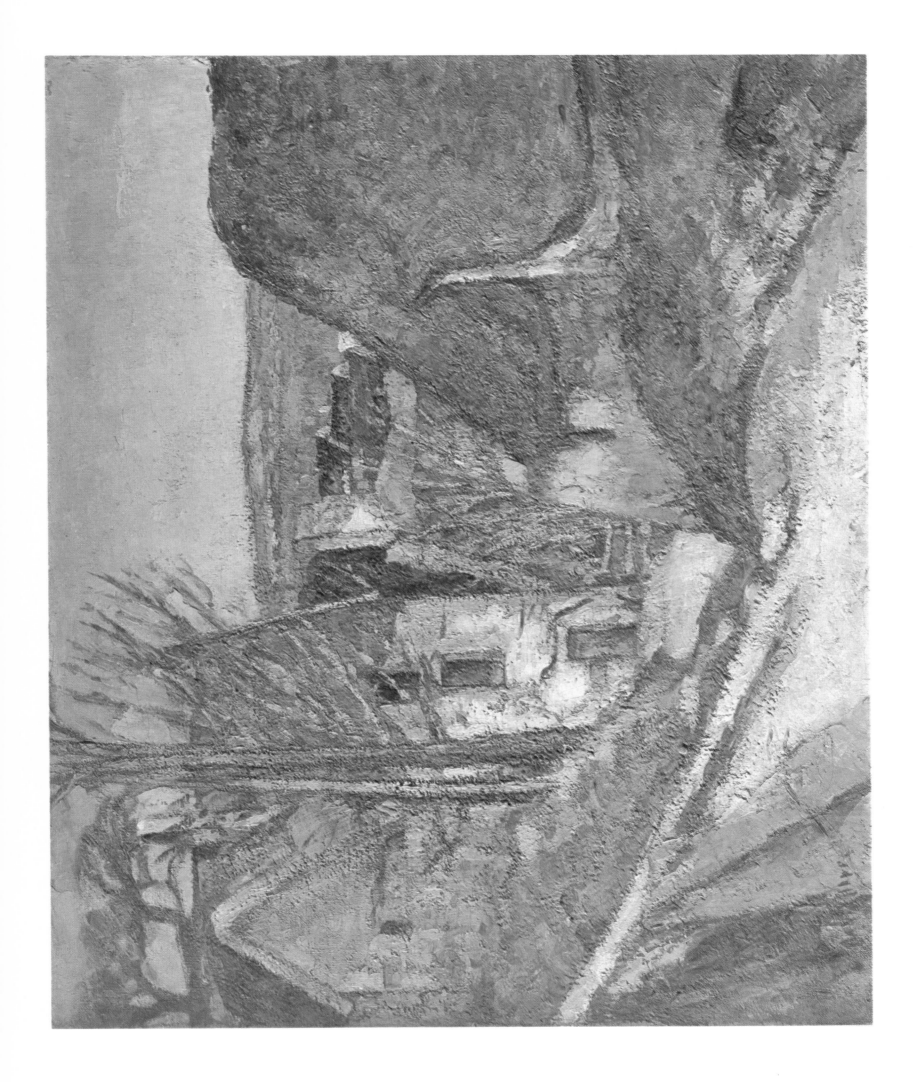

IV. THE CHATEAU OF MÉDAN (*c.* 1880)
Oil on canvas. 23¼ in. x 28⅜ in.
Glasgow Art Gallery and Museum (Burrell Collection)

During the early 1880's Cézanne made several visits to the country house at Médan, on the Seine near Paris, which his boyhood friend Zola had bought, enlarged and filled with luxurious artifacts and literary guests. Disliking the heavy meals and pompous company, Cézanne would often retreat to the river to paint. He sketched this scene from Zola's boat.

The Château of Médan (Zola's house is the red-shuttered, dormered building on the right) belongs to Cézanne's 'classical period', in which he masterfully combined the Impressionist handling of bright colour, soft shapes and broken brush strokes with his own sense of architectural structure. Insisting that a painting must maintain its two-dimensional integrity, he avoided the traditional devices of linear and aerial perspective used to create the illusion of depth. Here he readjusts nature to compose a painting of five static, horizontal bands: sky, trees, geometrically defined houses, river bank and water. The cool, recessively blue sky, overlapped by trees, stays behind the warm, projecting, orange river bank. At the same time, the bands are held together on one plane by the solid, tapestry-like effect of the short brush strokes. Diagonal in the trees and bushes, horizontal in the reflections in the water and patchily rectangular in the buildings, they achieve a unity through their rhythm, equality of size and intensity of colour.

V-VI. THE LARGE BATHERS (1898–1905)
Oil on canvas. 82 in. x 99 in.
Philadelphia Museum of Art (W. P. Wilstach Collection)

The subject of bathers, which has intrigued countless painters, occupied Cézanne for more than thirty years. Of his many studies of male and female bathers, this is the largest. He worked on it more than seven years, but it remained unfinished at his death.

Because it was too difficult to move an eight-foot canvas outdoors, Cézanne had to paint in his studio. Unable to obtain models locally, he worked from reproductions of masterworks and from his own drawings. Thus, the *Large Bathers* is one of his few paintings not based on direct observation.

Cézanne tried to integrate his figures into the landscape so that neither element would take precedence. In this firmly triangular composition two converging stands of trees and two groups of figures on a river bank frame a diamond-shaped vista of the far shore and sky. Unconcerned with the faces and sex of his bathers, the painter reduces them to geometric forms, a radical approach that soon influenced the Cubists. Overlaying patches of ochre, blue and green washes throughout the canvas in a loose, water-colour-like technique, Cézanne skillfully balances foreground and background, human figures and natural setting, to create a masterly whole.

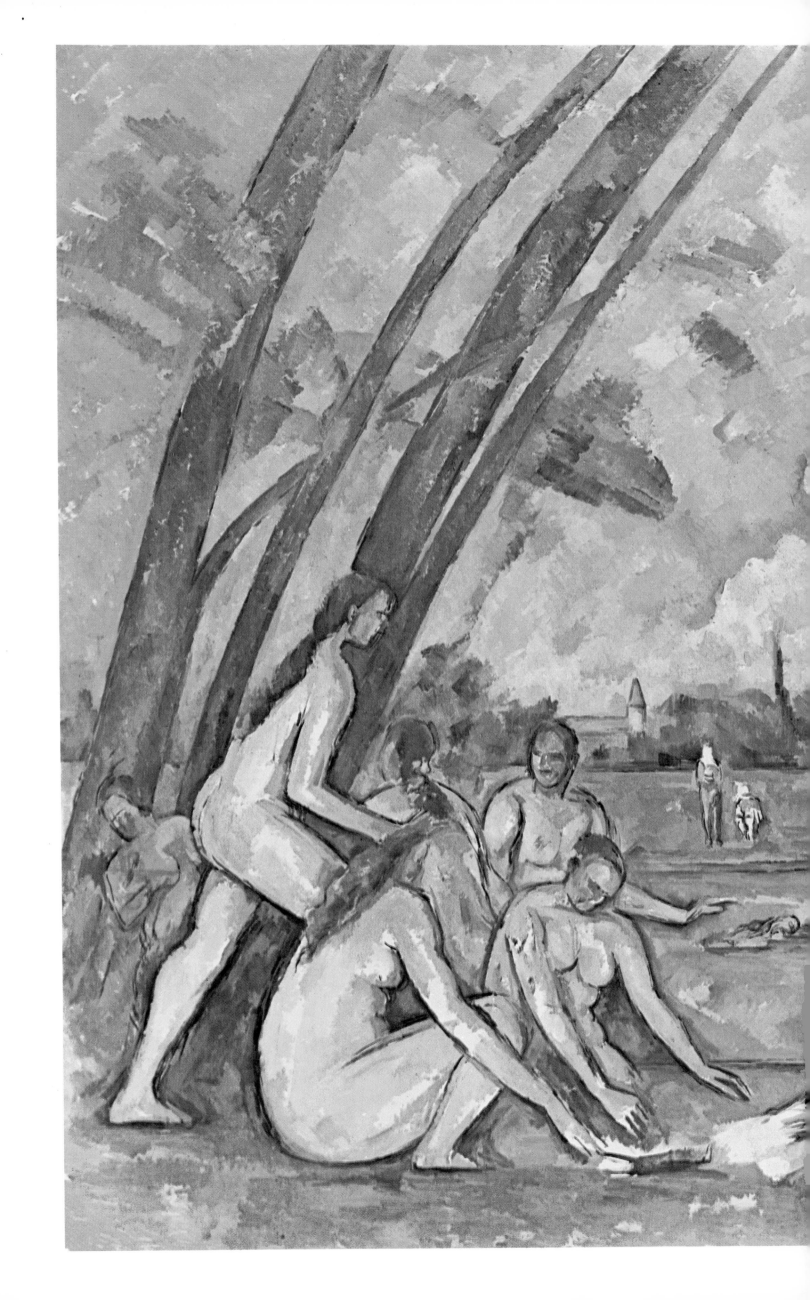

VII. THE GULF OF MARSEILLES SEEN FROM L'ESTAQUE (1883–85)
Oil on canvas. 28¾ in. x 39½ in.
Metropolitan Museum of Art, New York (Havemeyer Collection)

During the 1880's and 1890's Cézanne immersed himself in the study of the landscape of his native Provence. Feeling a 'sadness in Provence that no one has yet sung', he sought to understand its harsh, rocky structure revealed in strong, unchanging sunlight. The countryside around l'Estaque, with its orange-roofed houses and green trees intensified by the blue Mediterranean and distant hills, particularly attracted him.

Unlike many other views in which he tried to bring foreground and background into one decorative plane, in this work Cézanne uses colours—vibrant, assertive oranges close to the viewer and cool, recessive blues farther away—to create the effect of distance. He also stresses the parallel horizontal lines of the roof tops and of the far shore of the bay to provide breadth. Yet, in his characteristically controlled manner, he manages to balance these effects. He links foreground to background by making the sea a deep, solid body of pure colour rather than a shimmering surface. And he checks the sweeping horizontals with the curving shorelines of the middle ground and the strong vertical line of the foreground smokestack, repeated in nearby house chimneys.

VIII. MONT SAINTE-VICTOIRE (1885–87)
Oil on canvas. 26 in. x 35 in.
Courtauld Institute Galleries, London

One of Cézanne's favourite subjects was Mont Sainte-Victoire, the mountain he had known since boyhood that became the dominant subject in his landscapes from the mid-1880's on. In dozens of oils, watercolours and drawings he approached it from a variety of locations, always finding new ways to portray it. This is one of four versions done from his brother-in-law's estate at Montbriant. Cézanne gave it to the admiring young poet Joachim Gasquet, son of an old Aix friend.

According to Cézanne, 'Nature is made up of a series of curves and squares, which interlace'. Here, as usual, he painstakingly observes nature to find these relationships and reconstructs it to express them in an orderly work of art. The solidly structural bulk of the mountain rising above the wide sweep of the countryside is framed by the vertical pine tree trunk on the left and the fluid line of its outstretched branches, whose rhythmic curves repeat those of the horizon line. Although the shadowed tree trunk cutting through the middle ground and sky is clearly the closest object to the viewer, the soft tones of green, blue, ochre and rose distributed throughout the work tend to hold all the elements on one plane.

IX. MADAME CÉZANNE IN RED (1890–95)
Oil on canvas. 34¾ in. x 27½ in.
Museu de Arte, São Paulo

Cézanne painted and drew more than forty portraits of his mistress and wife, Hortense. From these likenesses she appears to have been a plain, well-built woman. According to his friends, who believed her mercenary and called her 'The Ball' (in the sense of ball and chain), she was a vivacious, superficial, conventional bourgeoise with no understanding of Cézanne's art. Certainly he often chose to be away from her, although the tie between them was lifelong. Perhaps he painted her so often because she was one of the few people, until his late years, who would patiently endure months of sittings and the artist's bad temper.

Although Cézanne said, 'The goal of all art is the human face', in this portrait, as in other works, he presents his subject with a cool detachment that is little concerned with recording the individuality of the sitter. Neither does it express the emotions of the painter but simply deals with the figure in space. Modifying the basic frontality of the pose, Cézanne shifts the body's axis slightly to the left, elevating the right shoulder and creating a rhythm that flows in an oval across her shoulder, down her left arm and through the curved hands in her lap. Her rich red dress stands out sharply against the soft, unbroken green background, yet touches of green are worked into the shadows of the face and hands.

X. STILL LIFE WITH BASKET OF APPLES (1890–95)
Oil on canvas. 25¾ in. x 32 in.
Art Institute of Chicago (Bartlett Memorial Collection)

Fascinated by the age-old problem of representing three-dimensional objects on a two-dimensional surface, Cézanne explored it in numerous still lifes, painting ordinary objects and fruits in apparently casual groupings. He was interested, however, not in recording components of domestic life but in creating a pictorial construction. Each object was carefully chosen for its simplicity of line or striking colour and then purposefully related to other objects and the background. Some things he propped up with blocks, books or coins (as, for example, the basket and cookie plate here) or tilted slightly off the vertical, as is the wine bottle. If a single object were moved or eliminated, the whole balance of the work would be disturbed.

Cézanne also adjusted shapes to suit pictorial needs. Here the cookie plate is squeezed into a narrow oblong, repeating the shape of the cookies. Both the back and front edges of the table are dislocated, creating tension. The soft white tablecloth is folded into shapes that are structurally more important to the composition than is the solid table. Its downthrusting, vertical foreground fold balances the upward thrust of the wine bottle. The crumpled cloth not only holds the apples together but, by covering the front of the table, prevents its discontinuity from unduly disturbing the viewer. Blurring the transition from the side of the table to the top, it weakens traditional depth perspective and so flattens out the picture space.

XI-XII. MONT SAINTE-VICTOIRE (1904–06)
Oil on canvas. 28⅞ in. x 36¼ in.
Philadelphia Museum of Art (Elkins Collection)

Ever dissatisfied with his efforts, Cézanne struggled unceasingly to reveal the truths of nature and arrange them as a work of art. In many of his late paintings of Mont Sainte-Victoire, such as this one, painted from above the studio he built on the Chemin des Lauves in Aix, he achieved brilliant success. This work pulses and glows as Cézanne, in old age and ill health, portrays his beloved countryside with a newfound freedom and exuberance.

Part of the work's vitality lies in the loose, patchy technique inspired by his watercolours. This technique is particularly effective in the subtle greens and blues of the sky, which seems not to lie behind the mountain but to stretch out along the same plane, and in the dark shades of the foreground that keep the bright middle ground from projecting too far. Part of the vitality lies in the tension Cézanne has created between the abstract and the particular. The forms of foliage, fields, houses and clouds have been so simplified and generalized as to become almost abstractions. Yet the looming presence of the mountain, whose planes and profile are clearly defined, allows them at the same time to remain recognizable symbols of real things. This tension, misunderstood by most of Cézanne's contemporaries, was later fruitfully explored by the Cubists, but vanished completely in nonobjective art.

XIII. THE OLD WOMAN WITH A ROSARY (*c.* 1895–96)
Oil on canvas. 31⅞ in. x 25¾ in.
National Gallery, London

Cézanne considered this late portrait a failure, perhaps because
he could not draw the left shoulder of the bowed figure to his
satisfaction. At any rate, he threw the finished canvas into a
corner, where it lay under a coal scuttle, dripped upon from a
zinc pipe, until his friend Gasquet later discovered it and kept it.
Gasquet spun a sentimental tale about the model, calling her a
'failed nun' who had fled her convent and whom Cézanne kindly
took into his service. In fact, she was the former servant of a
notary in Aix.

Structurally, the body of the old woman is ill-defined, the dark
shoulders barely distinguishable from the background. But the
frilled cap is crisply painted, and the full blue skirt is cheerful in
tone. The treatment of her submissively bowed head and gnarled
hands clutching the rosary, along with the powerful, expressive
brush strokes and sombre colours, reveals Cézanne's sympathetic
understanding of an old woman's patient acceptance of age and
infirmity.

XIV. ROCKS IN THE FOREST (1894–98)
Oil on canvas. 20⅛ in. x 24½ in.
Kunsthaus, Zurich

Cézanne's late works show a delicacy of touch far removed from his early work in thick impasto. He told Renoir, 'It took me forty years to find out that painting is not sculpture'. Yet his late landscapes such as this one, probably painted in the forest of Fontainebleau, have a solidity of construction that results on the one hand from carefully balanced composition and on the other from a painstaking building-up of thin layers of colour. Cézanne used colour not to fill in outlines, as the great draftsman Ingres had done, but, like the colourist Delacroix, to create forms. Holding that drawing and colour are inseparable, he interwove colour and line throughout his works, applying one over the other for a unity of effect.

For all its solidity, *Rocks in the Forest* also conveys a sense of movement. The slender trees spring rhythmically from the rocks. The angled brush strokes with which the rocks and foliage are rendered seem to make them vibrate. The sense of agitation in these late works may suggest a new, joyful spontaneity or the aging painter's growing awareness of the need to realize his aesthetic objectives while there was still time.

XV. STILL LIFE WITH PLASTER CUPID (*c.* 1895)
Oil on paper mounted on panel. 27½ in. x 22½ in.
Courtauld Institute Galleries, London

Two plaster casts in Cézanne's studio, a *Cupid* and a *Flayed Man*, which he erroneously attributed to the baroque sculptor Puget and to Michelangelo, respectively, appear in many of his still lifes. Here he juxtaposes them as symbolic opposites. The central *Cupid*, surrounded by apples and sprouting onions, stands for life. The *Flayed Man*, partially seen in the upper right corner, signifies the death that always shadows life. In his later years Cézanne was often preoccupied with thoughts of death, as evidenced by his many studies of skulls.

More important than its symbolism, perhaps, was the form of the *Cupid* and its function in the pictorial composition. Delighting in the curves of the figure, Cézanne repeats them in the roundness of the fruits and plays them against the rectangles of the canvases in the background. As the central element in the composition, the *Cupid* forms a strong vertical axis, twisted a little and tipped so as to be seen slightly from above. Its base is planted on the table top; its leg is superimposed on the sharply uptilted floor; and its torso is silhouetted against a leaning canvas on which it almost seems to be painted. Thus, it flattens out and unifies three different planes in this daringly complex late work.

XVI. STILL LIFE WITH APPLES AND ORANGES (1895–1900)
Oil on canvas. 29⅛ in. x 36⅝ in.
Louvre, Paris

Cézanne endowed his late works with a greater intensity of expression and complexity of design. Here he carefully interrelates the elements of the composition, making the simple, brilliant shapes of the fruits stand out against the white of the compote and the shadowed folds of the tablecloth but almost losing them in the richly patterned drapery behind. That fabric, in turn, seems to encroach on the flowered pitcher, which shares some of the white of the cloth. The warm, appealing colours are all in the upper half of the canvas, but interest in the lower half is maintained by the strong diagonal of the table edge and by the intricate folds of the linen.

The apples and oranges afford good examples of Cézanne's innovative modelling of form through colour. In place of the traditional chiaroscuro method of using highlights and shadows on one basic, descriptive hue, he composes an object of many tiny planes, or colour steps, each slightly different in angle and hue from its neighbour. Working from the darker outer edges where the turning away of the sphere creates its own outline, he moves with lighter, brighter tones towards the culminating central point closest to the viewer. Using fewer patches of pure colour on these late fruits, Cézanne moved further along the path from representation to abstraction without ever losing his grounding in observed reality.